IMAGES
of America

JAMESTOWN

During his long career as the editorial page cartoonist for the *Richmond Times-Dispatch*, Fred O. Seibel frequently reminded readers of Virginia's heritage and especially of the fact that Jamestown was settled before the colony of Massachusetts and is therefore the birthplace of the nation. The industrious crow in the lower left of this cartoon from the 1930s is a Seibel trademark.

IMAGES
of America

JAMESTOWN

Rodney B. Taylor and Will Molineux

ARCADIA
PUBLISHING

Published by Arcadia Publishing
Charleston SC, Chicago IL, Portsmouth NH, San Francisco CA

Library of Congress Catalog Card Number: 2004101355

For all general information contact Arcadia Publishing at:
Telephone 843-853-2070
Fax 843-853-0044
E-mail sales@arcadiapublishing.com
For customer service and orders:
Toll-Free 1-888-313-2665

Visit us on the Internet at www.arcadiapublishing.com

During the 1957 Jamestown Festival celebrating the 350th anniversary of the first permanent English settlement in America, Ronald K. Irving portrayed Capt. John Smith, the celebrated leader of the colony whose life was saved by in the Native princess Pocahontas. Irving, a navy captain, stands in front of the Smith statue on Jamestown Island. (Photo by Will Molineux.)

CONTENTS

ACKNOWLEDGMENTS

While there is a plentiful shelf of books about Jamestown's first century, there are few accounts of its next two and a half centuries, the years that America's birthplace was inert but not forgotten. Happily, Martha W. McCartney, a superb independent scholar of Virginia's early years, includes this era that has been skipped over—the period between 1699, when the capital of Virginia moved to Williamsburg, and 1892 when an association of ladies acquired the very spot where 104 brave Englishmen established their frontier settlement. McCartney's recent book *Jamestown: An American Legacy* is accurate, readable, and carries the story from 1607 to the present. She also is the author of the ever-useful *James City County: Keystone of The Commonwealth*. David F. Riggs, a National Park-Service historian, reminds us that Jamestown played a fairly significant role in the Civil War, although it was not the site of a battle. His engaging story is titled *Embattled Shrine: Jamestown in The Civil War*.

The preservation of Jamestown and the celebration of its importance are recorded in the history of the Association for the Preservation of Virginia Antiquities (APVA), *To Preserve and Protect*, by Richard T. Couture. Of help in recalling the Jamestown Festival of 1957 are the official reports of the federal and state commissions that staged the observance of the 350th anniversary of Jamestown. Officially, they were the Jamestown-Williamsburg-Yorktown Celebration Commission and the Virginia 350th Anniversary Commission. The commonwealth's investment in Jamestown Festival Park—now called Jamestown Settlement—was wise and has had an enduring impact on preserving the story of Jamestown, just as the APVA and the National Park Service have cooperated in preserving the island place now called Historic Jamestowne.

In the assembly of these photographs we are indebted to many persons. At the APVA we thank Elizabeth S. Kostelny, the association's executive secretary; Louis Malon, director of properties; Kathy Dean, curator of archives; and Jamie May, Ann Berry, and Michael Lavin, all members of the Jamestown Rediscovery staff. Once expenses of this effort have been covered, profits will be donated to the APVA.

Thanks also to Jane Sundberg and David Riggs of the Colonial National Historical Park; Stephanie A.T. Jacobe, visual resources manager of the Virginia Historical Society; Teresa E. Roane, director of archives and photographic services of the Valentine Museum at the Richmond History Center; Maryann Martin of the John D. Rockefeller Jr. Library of the Colonial Williamsburg Foundation; Debby Padgett and Tracy Perkins, media relations managers for the Jamestown-Yorktown Foundation; Audrey Johnson, picture collection coordinator of the Library of Virginia; and Wayne Dementi of Dementi Studios in Richmond. Those individuals who permitted us use of their personal photographs are acknowledged in credit lines accompanying the appropriate captions.

We appreciate the support and encouragement we have received from Susan E. Beck, editor of Arcadia's *Image of America* series, and our wives, Dolly Taylor and Mary Sawyer Molineux.

INTRODUCTION

In 1607 the English frontier in America was Jamestown. A century later the capital of Virginia was moved to Williamsburg, and the frontier had moved across the Piedmont to the foothills of the Blue Ridge Mountains. Jamestown gave Virginia—and English America—its start, but at the end of the 17th century its population was less than it was when 104 men built James Fort.

Jamestown was not abandoned. A few brick houses were occupied and ferries and riverboats still landed there. A tobacco inspection warehouse was there until the American Revolution. Until the mid-1700s church services were held in the 1639 sanctuary with its sturdy bell tower. The strategically located island was fortified during the War of 1812 and the Revolutionary War. Troops under Cornwallis occupied the island when a detachment of American riflemen under Lafayette clashed with British dragoons at nearby Green Springs in July 1781. Two months later French troops landed at Jamestown and marched to Yorktown.

According to historian Martha McCartney, ownership of town lots was "absorbed" during the 18th century by two families, the Jaquelins and Travises, whose fields were tended by slave labor. In the mid-18th century Richard Ambler, who married into the Jaquelin family, built a mansion where Jamestown's New Town had stood. The ruins of that landmark remain today.

A passing diarist in 1777 noted of the church that "ruins only remain" and "tall trees grow in the churchyard which serve as haunt for blackbirds and crows, and add to the Gloom of the Prospect." By colonial law, ownership of the vacated church and graveyard reverted to the General Assembly. The church tower erected in 1647 is the only remaining 17th-century structure above ground at Jamestown.

Throughout colonial times and well into 19th century, Jamestown was not a true island because it was accessible upstream by a shallow isthmus that eventually washed away. In 1833 two entrepreneurs built a wooden bridge over Back River and a causeway through a marsh on the mainland side. This bridge was washed out by a storm during the 1840s and replaced. New bridges were built in 1897 and in 1918. The Hurricane of 1933 again isolated the island and the bridge was rebuilt. The last bridge was removed before the 1957 Jamestown Festival, when the Colonial Parkway was extended from Williamsburg to Jamestown over a man-made isthmus.

In 1861 Gen. Robert E. Lee ordered the construction of several earthen redoubts on the island. The main one was Fort Pocahontas, built by the old church tower and, as archaeological investigations have uncovered, on top of a portion of the 1607 James Fort. Confederate ordnance officers tested cannon and iron plating that was to be mounted on the CSS *Virginia* tested at Jamestown. After May 1862 Union forces occupied Jamestown as an important communications post.

After the Civil War the island was owned by a succession of farmers. The small plot of land where the old church tower stood attracted the interest of a group of heritage-minded ladies who in 1889 organized as the Association for the Preservation of Virginia Antiquities. On March 1, 1892, the General Assembly granted the APVA the deed to the church site and a right of way across the island. Later that year the island was acquired by Edward Barney, an Ohio industrialist who had made his wealth building railroad cars. Barney also headed a James River steamship line and built a 200-foot wharf at Jamestown. On May 13, 1893, the 286th anniversary of the landing at Jamestown, Barney gave the APVA 22.5 acres around the church tower and including Fort Pocahontas. The roadway between the Back River bridge and the Barney Wharf on the James River went through the APVA property and passed immediately in front of the old church tower.

At that time it was thought that the site of James Fort had been washed away by the tidal river. To hold the shoreline in place, Barney and the APVA agreed to build a seawall, a project that was carried out by army engineers in 1901 with a $40,000 congressional appropriation. Two leaders of the APVA made preliminary archaeological digs to locate the foundations of the 1639 church and the supervisor of the seawall construction, Samuel H. Yonge, undertook the first published study of old "James Towne."

In 1807 a Jamestown Jubilee was held and another in 1822. For the 250th anniversary in 1857, a 500-seat dining hall was erected and a speaker's platform for President John Tyler. There was a military review, dancing, and "every variety of gambling . . . in full blast." The celebrants—who came aboard 13 steamboats and several schooners—chipped souvenirs from tombstones and carried off bricks from the church site. President Tyler's son, Lyon G. Tyler, president of the College of William and Mary, inaugurated annual observances of May 13 in 1888.

A memorable celebration was held in 1907 when several patriotic organizations contributed substantially to the APVA's development of the historic place. The National Society of Colonial Dames built a Memorial Church over the foundations of the 1639 church and the National Society of the Daughters of the American Revolution built a hospitality house, later called the Yeardley House. The federal government erected a 103-foot commemorative obelisk. In 1908 an impressive statue of Capt. John Smith was erected, and in 1922 a statue of Pocahontas was unveiled as well as the Hunt Shrine, commemorating the first Communion service celebrated at Jamestown. The 1957 Jamestown Festival featured visits by Queen Elizabeth II, Vice President Richard M. Nixon, and 1.2 million people. Virginia built a museum park a mile upstream from the island. Now called Jamestown Settlement, it features reproductions of James Fort, a Native-American lodge, and the three ships that brought the first Jamestown settlers, the *Susan Constant*, *Godspeed*, and *Discovery*. In 1934 the National Park Service acquired the remainder of Jamestown Island from Barney's widow, Louise, and since 1940 the APVA and the National Park Service have administered America's birthplace.

Although Jamestown—now Historic Jamestowne—attracts more than 500,000 a year, only a few families live there. One of them is Bill and Vivian Smith and their son Rodney Taylor, who grew up on the island during World War II. His personal story is told in Chapter Seven, "Rodney Remembers."

One

OLD TOWER CHURCH

To many Virginians, the old church tower on Jamestown Island is a "most sacred relic." It is the only remaining evidence above ground of the abandoned 17th-century colonial capital of Virginia, and was acquired in 1892 by the APVA along with surrounding acreage on the eroding shoreline of the James River. (Courtesy of APVA Preservation Virginia.)

When this photograph—the oldest picture of the old church tower—was taken in 1852, Jamestown Island was owned by William Allen, one of the wealthiest men in Virginia, who lived upriver at Claremont. His farm manager and 50 slaves cultivated wheat, corn, and oats, and looked after 250 cattle, sheep, and hogs. (Courtesy of Dementi Studio, Richmond.)

The brick tower was built around 1647 as an addition to a sanctuary erected in 1639. It is approximately 18 feet square with walls three feet thick at the base. Originally, the tower was about 46 feet tall and had two upper floors, with the top one probably serving as a lookout post. (Courtesy of APVA Preservation Virginia.)

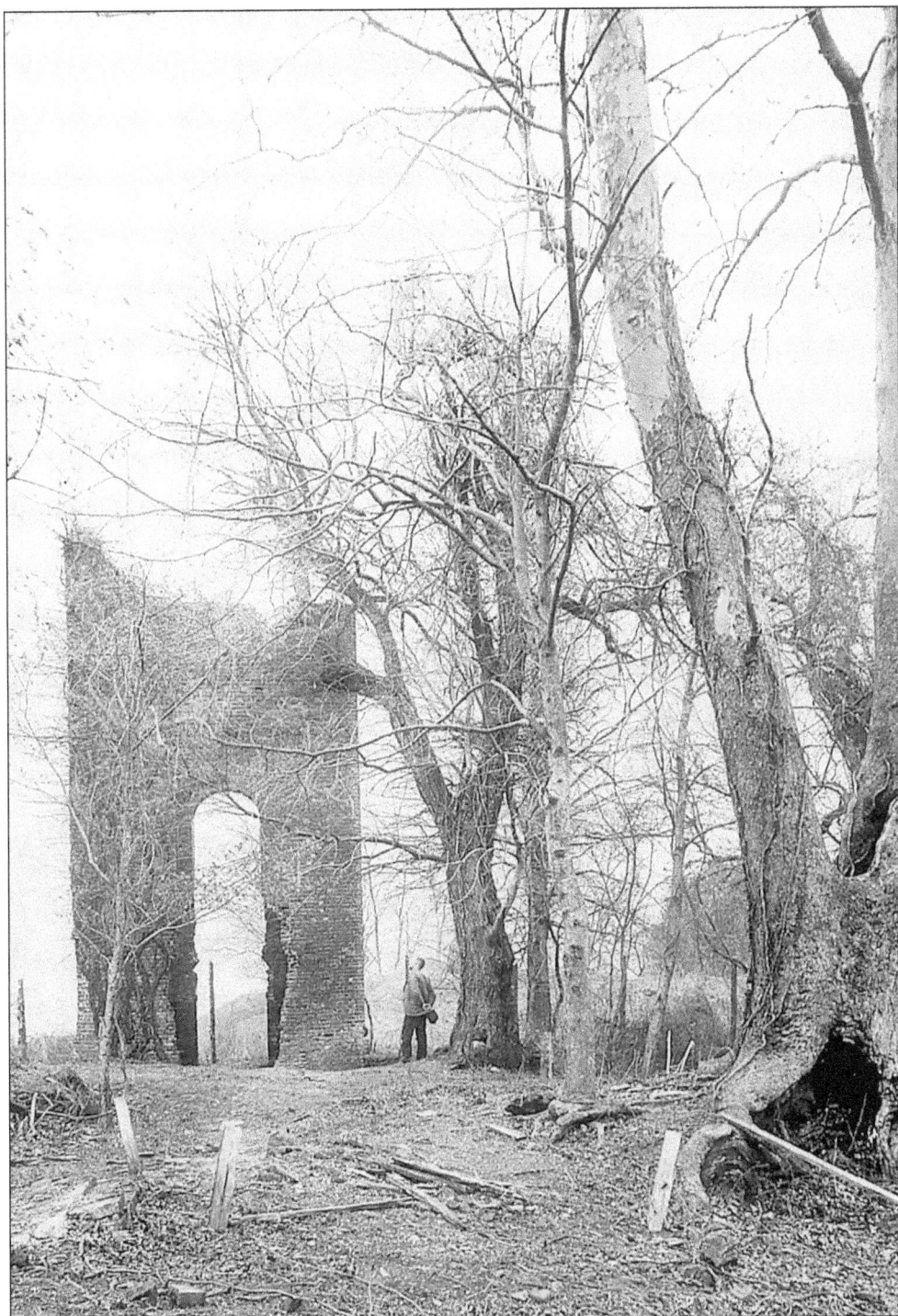

The old church tower, seen here from the sanctuary side, always has been a point of curiosity. Edward E. Barney, a wealthy industrialist from Ohio who owned the island in 1892 as well as a steamship company, considered building a hotel and making Jamestown Island a tourist attraction. (Courtesy of APVA Preservation Virginia.)

The Virginia General Assembly, which controlled the abandoned church tower and graveyard, conveyed the historic property to the APVA on March 1, 1892. A year later Barney and his wife Louise gave the APVA 22.5 adjoining acres. The unattractive barbed-wire fence was put up to protect the site from relic hunters. (Courtesy of APVA Preservation Virginia.)

Archaeological investigations of the church were begun by two APVA members, Mary Jeffrey Galt and Mary W. Garrett. They cleared away vegetation and debris and discovered two separate foundations—an outer foundation of brick and an inner one of cobblestones. (Courtesy of APVA Preservation Virginia.)

Mary Jeffrey Galt of Norfolk, who along with Cynthia Beverley Tucker Coleman of Williamsburg founded the APVA, reported in 1897 that she "dug with [her] own hands quite deep" into the foundations. Later excavations uncovered the brick floor and several tombs, including one of a knight. (Courtesy of APVA Preservation Virginia.)

13

The foundations of the church were capped and iron rods installed to strengthen the tower walls, although weeds appear to be growing from the top of the tower. This photograph was taken in connection with the 1907 Jamestown Exposition. (Courtesy of the Library of Virginia.)

To protect the foundations of the church the APVA erected a temporary wooden shelter in 1901 that is faintly visible to the right of the tower in this postcard view. Although the wire fence remains, the APVA had taken steps to improve the historic grounds.

The National Society of Colonial Dames in 1908 replaced the shelter with the brick Memorial Church, designed by a Boston architect to conform to "American church architecture "of the earliest colonial period." Bricks salvaged from two old buildings in Hampton, Virginia, were used.

Inside the Memorial Church visitors can see the foundation of the 1617 church made from ships' ballast stones and the outer brick foundations of the 1639 church. This view shows the tombs in the graveyard at the east side of the church.

Along the interior walls of the church memorial plaques honor individuals such as Chanco, the Native-American boy who in 1622 warned the Jamestown settlers of an impending massacre; John Pott, the physician; Thomas Savage, "gentlemen and ensign;" George Sandys, "the first American poet;" the colonial governors; and "The Common Law."

Rev. William Archer Rutherfoord Goodwin, rector of Bruton Parish Church whose vision led to the restoration of Williamsburg, was an active member of the APVA and on several occasions conducted worship services in what came to be called the Old Tower Church.

16

Stonemasons resealed the cement cap on the old tower in the spring of 1952, at a time when the APVA's road was still open to automobiles. (Courtesy of the National Park Service.)

In the graveyard a sycamore tree grew up between the tombs of Rev. James Blair, the Anglican commissary of Virginia and founder of the College of William and Mary, and his wife Sarah Harrison Blair. Because her parents thought Blair too old and opposed the marriage, the tree that separates their graves is called the Mother-in-Law Tree.

For many years Sam Robinson lived on Jamestown Island and was the guide at the Old Tower Church. He was noted for his rapid-fire account of colonial times and especially his own unique interpretation of the Mother-in-Law Tree. (Courtesy of Rodney Taylor.)

Two

THE APVA

For almost 30 years—from 1929 until 1957—these two L-shaped piers served Jamestown. A three-masted sailing schooner and a barge are tied up at the ferry pier, built by Edward Barney in 1893. The empty wharf was built by the federal government in 1929 for excursion boats. The road inland to Williamsburg—State Route 31 that crosses over Back River—passes along side the Tercentenary Monument. Both piers were removed prior to the 1957 Jamestown Festival. (Courtesy of the Library of Virginia.)

Old Tower Church, center, is almost hidden in this aerial view taken in the early 1920s, while the Tercentenary Monument of 1907 commands attention. The Yeardly House, the APVA's Jamestown headquarters with its enclosed rose garden, is at the upper left, and directly in front of it, at the shoreline, is the Rest House, later called the Relic House. The main gate to the

APVA grounds is near the downstream terminus of the seawall. The second gate is directly above it along the horizontal tree line marking the APVA boundary. The bridge across Back River is at the upper right. (Courtesy of APVA Preservation Virginia.)

A concrete seawall built in 1901 and four wooden breakwaters protect the island's downstream shoreline. The foundations of a row house, sections of which served as two 17th-century statehouses, are to the left perpendicular to the seawall and in front of the Yeardly House. The APVA's Relic House is across the vale at the first breakwater. The cluster of trees above it

obscures the Old Tower Church and a Civil War earthwork erected by the Confederates in 1861 called Fort Pocahontas. The straight road heads away from the ferry pier downstream to Black Point at the island's eastern end. (Courtesy of the National Park Service.)

Visitors arriving aboard a James River steamboat approached Jamestown from the Government Pier that leads directly toward the imposing Tercentenary Monument, erected by the United States government in 1907. Downstream to the right is an open well house; at the left is the APVA gatehouse. (Courtesy of Colonial Williamsburg.)

The artesian well, spewing forth at the extreme left, was dug at the riverbank between the two wharfs to provide water for buildings on the island as well as refreshment for visitors. Souvenirs were available at the waiting shelter for the ferry. The wooden jetty is one of four breakwaters. (Courtesy of the National Park Service.)

The square brick gatehouse was built in 1929 by the APVA and also served as a federal post office. Visitors would go to the ticket window to pay the modest admission fee, pass through a turnstile and then the gate at the right. For a few years before it was demolished in 1960 attorney John Alcott occupied the gatehouse.

This postcard from the 1930s shows the sign to the right of the APVA's main gate that reads: "APVA Grounds. Admission 25 cents. Open Sunday 1 p.m. to 5 p.m." The statue of Pocahontas facing up the James River is to the immediate right of the path leading to the statue of Capt. John Smith. This wrought iron gate was relocated north of the Old Tower Church prior to 1957.

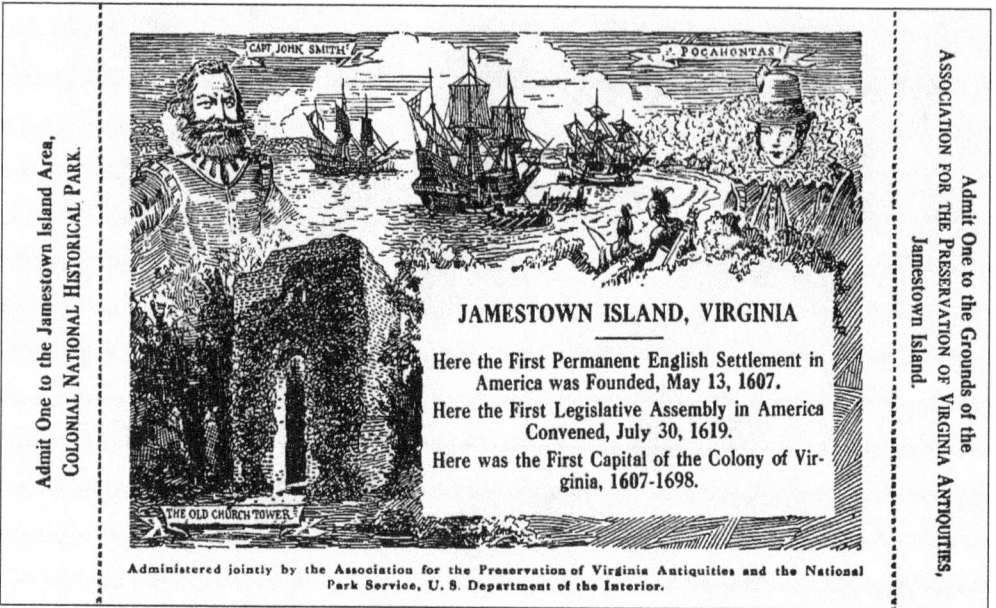

CAPT JOHN SMITH

POCAHONTAS

JAMESTOWN ISLAND, VIRGINIA

Here the First Permanent English Settlement in America was Founded, May 13, 1607.

Here the First Legislative Assembly in America Convened, July 30, 1619.

Here was the First Capital of the Colony of Virginia, 1607-1698.

THE OLD CHURCH TOWER

Administered jointly by the Association for the Preservation of Virginia Antiquities and the National Park Service, U. S. Department of the Interior.

This ticket, which could also be used as a postcard, admitted the bearer to both the APVA grounds and to the National Park Service Archaeological Museum. The tag at the right was removed by the APVA and the left tag by the NPS. Beginning in 1957 the entrance to the island was moved to Glasshouse Point on the Colonial Parkway and manned by Park Service personnel.

The APVA's other gate, to the north or landward side of the APVA grounds, was also erected in 1907 when the association's property was enclosed by a protective fence. This gateway, which still stands, leads to the Old Tower Church by way of the Yeardley House. Both gates were gifts of the Colonial Dames.

26

Just inside the APVA's main gate are two stone-mounted bronze markers. On the left is a tribute to Edward and Louise Barney for their gift of historic land, and to the right is a marker commemorating the landing of French troops under Marquis de St. Simon in 1781 for the siege of Cornwallis at Yorktown. The weathervane at the top of the gatehouse is—incongruously—a figure of Peter Stuyvesant, the peg-legged 17th-century Dutch governor of New York. (Courtesy of the National Park Service.)

General View of the A. P. V. A. Grounds
Jamestown Island, Virginia

Past the entrance gate the layout of several monuments between the river and the Old Tower Church becomes clear. Pocahontas faces upstream and to her far right is a monument to the House of Burgesses. The cross was erected by the Episcopal Church and in the distance at the riverbank is the statue of Capt. John Smith.

When the bronze statue of Pocahontas, daughter of the great chief Powhatan, was unveiled in 1922 it stood alone on the APVA grounds. In 1957 it was taken off its granite pedestal and moved to its present location north of the Old Tower Church. (Courtesy of APVA Preservation Virginia.)

Money raised by the APVA for the Pocahontas memorial, designed by William Ordway Partridge, was supplemented by an appropriation from Congress. Under the crossed arrows are the dates of her life, 1595–1617. From this perspective, the main gate is at the right. (Courtesy of APVA Preservation Virginia.)

The Norfolk branch of the APVA provided this House of Burgesses monument in 1907 to commemorate the first representative legislative body in the New World. The House convened at Jamestown on July 30, 1619. On it are the names of the burgesses who represented settlements on the James River. William A. Anderson, Virginia's attorney general, and two Episcopal bishops participated in the dedicatory ceremony.

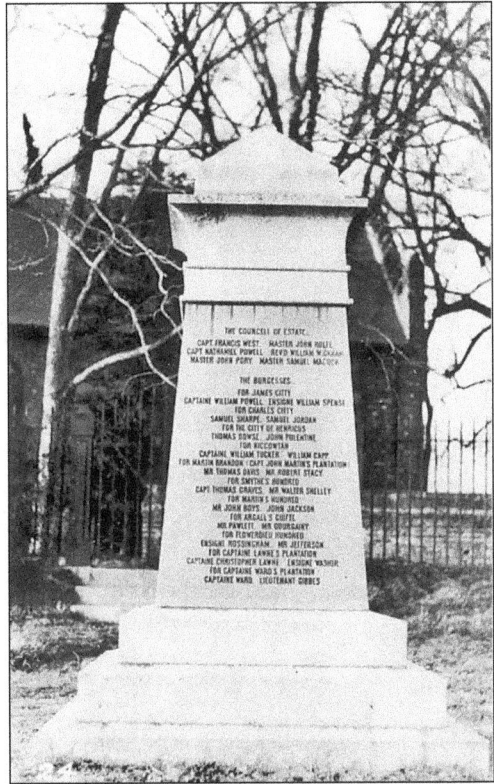

The general convention of the Episcopal Church, in session in Washington, D.C., convened on Jamestown Island on October 15, 1898, to celebrate the establishment of the Anglican faith in America. As a result of that assembly, this granite cross was placed near the Old Tower Church. The path leads through Fort Pocahontas.

Joseph Bryan, a wealthy Richmond businessman and newspaper publisher, and his wife Isobel, donated this statue of Capt. John Smith sculpted by William Couper of Norfolk and New York City. It was unveiled May 13, 1909, by their grandson, Joseph Bryan III, before a crowd that arrived aboard steamships from Richmond and Norfolk. (Courtesy of the Library of Virginia.)

As Capt. John Smith, considered by many the Father of Virginia, looks out upon the James River, the statue of Pocahontas, in the distance and surrounded by visitors, looks toward him. To the right of the gate, a car drives off the ferry pier.

In his right hand Capt. John Smith holds a book representing his writings about Virginia, while his left hand rests on his sword. The inscription says "Captain John Smith Governor of Virginia 1608." In the background is the iron fence around the Old Tower Church.

The statute of Capt. John Smith always has been a favorite subject of photographers, even during a winter snowstorm in 1940. The cleared roadway passes in front of the Old Tower Church. The gentle embankment is Fort Pocahontas. (Photo by Rodney Taylor.)

31

The memorial to commemorate the first celebration by Jamestown settlers of Holy Communion frames a bronze bas-relief depicting that 1607 service with two 16-foot-high brick pillars supporting a sandstone segmental arch. Originally, the shrine, shown here displaying 17th-century Communion silver, stood near the riverbank with its back to the water on part of Fort Pocahontas that had been leveled. (Courtesy of APVA Preservation Virginia.)

In 1960 the shrine, named for the colony's first chaplain Rev. Robert Hunt, was rolled across the interior of Fort Pocahontas and repositioned facing toward the river on the inward side of the northern embankment where it takes advantage of a small amphitheatre setting. Ralph Adams Cram, who at that time was America's premier Gothic Revival architect, designed the shrine in 1922. (Courtesy of Colonial Williamsburg.)

On the upriver side of Fort Pocahontas is one of several wells dug on Jamestown Island. Prior to 1907 the interior of the fort was drained and graded "to make the place healthy and orderly." A caretaker's cottage once stood on this site. The pathway leads to brick steps in front of the Hunt Shrine where it was sited before 1960.

This "Memorial Drinking Fountain" was placed in 1907 on the landward side of Fort Pocahontas beside the road through the APVA property midway between the two gates. The Society of Colonial Wars provided the fountain for "ample drinking water for man and beast." Note the tin cup sitting at the left side of the bowl. (Courtesy of the Virginia Historical Society, Richmond.)

The Yeardley House—originally called the Memorial House—was built by the National Society of the Daughters of the American Revolution as a hospitality house for the Jamestown Exposition. It was not completed until the end of 1907, the year this picture was taken. (Courtesy of Mary Helms.)

Of 17th-century English design, the Yeardley House supposedly was styled after the birthplace of Sir Walter Raleigh in Devonshire. It is named for Sir George Yeardley, the colonial governor who, in 1619, called the first legislation session of representatives from 11 settlements in Virginia. The rose garden, with each bush representing a state, was a principal feature of the APVA's beautification plan.

In front of the Yeardley House and across the vale is the Rest House, built in 1907. It was later known as the Relic House and, in more recent years, as the Thomas Dale House. For years it was the APVA's souvenir house where artifacts from the 1900–1903 excavations were displayed. The road through the APVA grounds winds around Fort Pocahontas, overgrown with trees. (Courtesy of APVA Preservation Virginia.)

Perpendicular to the riverbank and upstream from the Relic House are the foundations of Virginia's third and fourth statehouses, which have been extensively investigated by archaeologists. The fourth statehouse accidentally burned in 1698 and Virginia's capital was relocated to Williamsburg. The roof of the Yeardley House is seen beyond the English flag. (Courtesy of APVA Preservation Virginia.)

In 1957, the presiding bishop of the Episcopal Church in the United States, the Right Reverend Henry Knox Sherill, dedicated this large wooden cross erected by the APVA to mark the graves of early settlers, many of whom died during the Starving Time of 1609–1610. The graves, located near the 17th-century Virginia statehouse, were uncovered by National Park Service archaeologists in 1954–1955. (Photo by Rodney Taylor.)

One of the chief priorities of the APVA was to stabilize the riverbank. Foundations at the southernmost section of the statehouse complex already had tumbled onto the beach and into the river. It was long thought that the lone cypress tree marked the 17th-century shoreline and that Fort James of 1607 had been washed away. (Courtesy of APVA Preservation Virginia.)

Federal funds helped pay for the cement seawall built in1901 under the direction Col. Samuel H. Yonge of the Army Corps of Engineers. The sign notes that the settlers' "landing place" is 160 yards offshore. Recent archaeological studies sponsored by the APVA and directed by William M. Kelso prove the site of the 1607 James Fort was not washed away. (Courtesy of the Virginia Historical Society, Richmond.)

This view of the newly built seawall looks downstream and shows the pier with warehouse built by Edward E. Barney. The building at the left inside Fort Pocahontas was a caretaker's cottage. (Courtesy of the Virginia Historical Society, Richmond.)

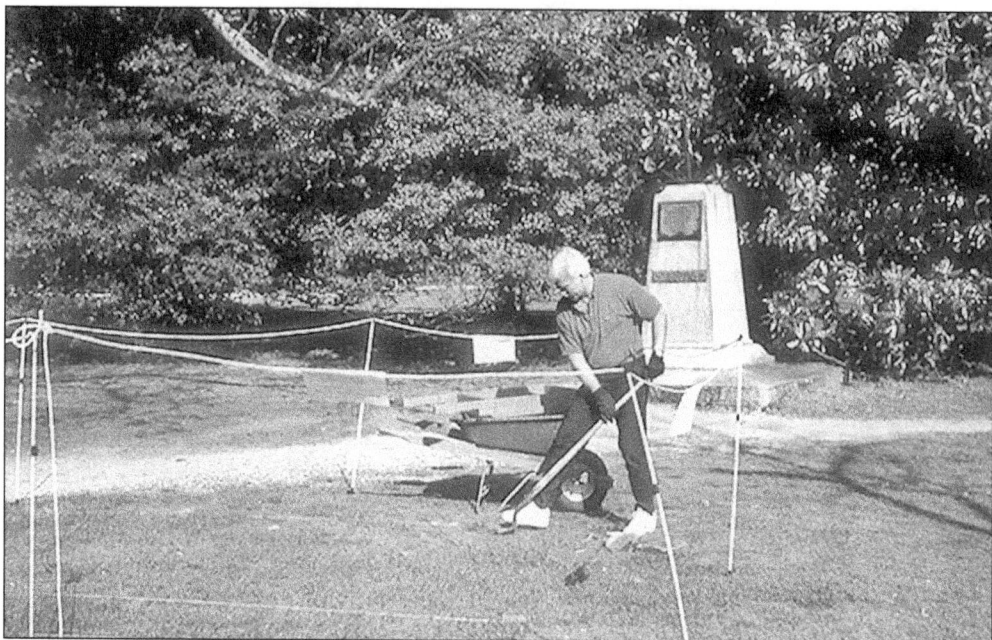

On April 4, 1994, Dr. William M. Kelso put the first spade in the ground to inaugurate the APVA's archaeological excavation to determine if there is evidence on land of the triangular James Fort. Behind him is the granite base of the Pocahontas monument which, at that time, held the repositioned bronze plaque to the French troops of 1781. It has since been removed. (Courtesy of APVA Preservation Virginia.)

After a little more than two years of digging, Kelso and his team of APVA archaeologists found the imprint of the fort's palisade wall that roughly paralleled the James River and the downstream bulwark. Public announcement of the historic discovery was made on September 12, 1996. (Courtesy of APVA Preservation Virginia.)

Subsequent excavations led to the discovery of buildings just outside the palisade on the downstream side of the fort. Here Seth Mallios, left, and Heather Lapham are working in the cellar of a post-fort building. (Photo by Rodney Taylor.)

Evidence of a 1640 warehouse and residence that belonged to John White was uncovered in 1998 after the downstream bulwark of the fort was located and studied. The APVA gatehouse and post office had stood on this very spot. (Photo by Rodney Taylor.)

Faint but conclusive evidence of the James Fort can be seen in this keystone-shaped excavation near Old Tower Church, to the left. The palisade runs in a line between the two archaeologists and straight across the exposed area to the right and under the tree-covered embankment of Fort Pocahontas. The separate indentations expose evidence of fence posts and other features. The roadway through the APVA property passed over this excavation. (Courtesy of APVA Preservation Virginia, photo by Michael Lavin.)

Three

THE NATIONAL PARK SERVICE

The tip of the Tercentenary Monument rises above the treetops and dominates the skyline along Jamestown Island's southern shore and, since it was erected in 1907, is a landmark for all who sail on the James River. The island, now designated Historic Jamestowne, is administered under a 1940 joint agreement between the APVA and the National Park Service. (Courtesy of APVA Preservation Virginia.)

The spot on which the Tercentenary Monument stands was given to the federal government by the APVA. In 1934, the federal government acquired the remainder of the island, approximately 1,500 acres of wood and marshland. For it, Louise Barney was awarded $165,000. (Courtesy of APVA Preservation Virginia.)

The federal government appropriated $50,000 for this obelisk patterned after the Washington Monument to commemorate the 300th anniversary of Jamestown. It is made of New Hampshire granite and rises 103 feet above the base. (Courtesy of APVA Preservation Virginia.)

In the summer of 1932 the monument was repaired and cleaned. The steps at the base of the shaft were covered by dirt when the National Park Service built its visitor center nearby for the 350th anniversary celebration. (Courtesy of the National Park Service.)

Motorists from Southside Virginia drove off the ferry pier and headed straight toward a building that served southbound travelers as a waiting room and souvenir shop. New Towne—where after the 1620s colonists built homes along marl pathways—is downstream to the right, as is the ruin of the 18th-century Ambler House. (Courtesy of the National Park Service.)

In 1934 the National Park Service initiated archaeological studies and improved visitor facilities. The waiting shelter for the ferry was remodeled and a comfort station, right, was built. The APVA grounds are to the left of the Tercentenary Monument. (Courtesy of the National Park Service.)

When the National Park Service next expanded its building, giving it a more box-like appearance, it installed a soda fountain and lunch counter, making it a gathering place for rural residents from off the island. Nearby a small museum was constructed. (Courtesy of the National Park Service.)

Gathered for the June 1, 1938, opening of the National Park Service's museum are, from left to right, B. Floyd Flickinger, superintendent of the Colonial National Historical Park; J.C. Harrington, the park service's principal on-site archaeologist; Virginia H. Sutton, an archaeologist and ranger; Gordon Myers, the resident ranger; and museum project manager, Mr. Vandervoort. (Courtesy of the National Park Service.)

This modest home was built not far from the National Park Service's visitor assembly area and in 1938 was occupied by Gordon Myers, the resident ranger. (Courtesy of the National Park Service.)

One of the more unusual incidents park service rangers were called to investigate was this automobile that had been driven across the sandy beach at Black Point and found after midnight on December 30, 1937. Their report indicates the car's owner was a man from Fairfax, Virginia. (Courtesy of the National Park Service.)

Work crews of the Civil Conservation Corps were quartered on Jamestown Island and the two men in this 1937 photograph are constructing a tool shed that also housed a fire truck. (Courtesy of the National Park Service.)

The National Park Service's fire truck was equipped with a small gasoline-powered pump and rather large water tank and was suitable for extinguishing fires in the island's woods and marshland. (Courtesy of the National Park Service.)

To stabilize the riverbank below the APVA's seawall, the National Park Service brought huge boulders by barge and used a crane to put them in position. This work was underway in the spring of 1935. (Courtesy of the National Park Service.)

Much of the work the CCC crews performed was clearing brush, cutting firewood, and maintaining a picnic area in a grove of pecan trees near the New Towne "high way." The leader of this crew in the winter of 1935 was a man named Chapman. (Courtesy of the National Park Service.)

National Park Service archaeologists, digging along the riverbank in the New Towne area, uncovered the remains of a 17th-century kiln used to make mortar and plaster from oyster shells. The iron bands supported the shells as they were heated by a wood fire in the brick-lined firebox below. (Courtesy of the Library of Virginia.)

Jean Carl "Pinky" Harrington, an archaeologist with the National Park Service at Jamestown from 1934 until 1941, uncovered the glasshouse of 1608 and the foundations of buildings in the New Towne area. In so doing, he recovered a vast array of Native-American arrowheads and other artifacts. (Courtesy of APVA Preservation Virginia.)

49

The National Park Service undertook extensive archaeological investigation of the base of the 17th-century statehouses on the APVA grounds in 1955. Here, with their trowels, are John L. Cotter, left, and Edward B. Jelks. (Courtesy of the Library of Virginia.)

Among others who took part in archaeology was Carl Younglove, at the left, in one of the basements of the statehouse group. Among the many jobs Younglove held were groundskeeper, gift shop clerk, ferryboat engineer, and lunch counter manager. The man with the shovel is unidentified. (Courtesy of Rodney Taylor.)

J. Paul Hudson, here with a dirt-encrusted metal object that had just been dug up, was a National Park Service museum curator and archaeologist at Jamestown for 25 years, and author of articles on glass and ceramics for scholarly journals. He also was a historian of the Episcopal Church in Virginia. (Photo by Will Molineux.)

One of the skilled laboratory technicians who worked with the National Park Service archaeologists was Berley Green, here cementing together pottery fragments. (Courtesy of the Library of Virginia.)

Sometime well before the National Park Service began making improvements to the island, maple trees were planted flanking the New Towne "high way" just downstream from the Barney ferry pier. It was a favorite picnic spot at the turn of the century.

This postcard view of Maple Drive was published by B.E. Steel, who leased land from Louise Barney and operated a park in the 1920s. Reportedly, Steel operated a bathhouse and snack bar.

In the mid-18th century, when Jamestown Island had essentially been abandoned and crops grew right up to the Old Tower Church, Richard Ambler built a substantial home overlooking the James River. This undated postcard erroneously states that it was the residence of a colonial governor.

The Ambler House was plundered by the British in the War of 1812, occupied by Confederate officers during the Civil War, burned by a slave uprising in 1862, and was later repaired and occupied by George W. Bedell, who managed the Barney's farm, until a fire gutted it in 1895.

When the National Park Service built the scenic five-mile-long Loop Road through the woods and marshes of the downstream end of Jamestown Island in 1957, an outdoor gallery of roadside interpretive paintings was set up at pull-offs. The paintings, done by Sidney King, depict life in colonial Jamestown, such as the enlarged inset of lumbering. (Courtesy of Thomas L. Williams.)

Four

FERRIES AND STEAMBOATS

In 1893 Edward Barney built this pier to accommodate steamships bringing freight, mail, and excursionists to Jamestown, and in 1923 it was leased to B.E. Steel who, for a decade, operated a park for picnickers and sold souvenirs. When Alfred F. Jester began his ferry service between Jamestown and Surry County he docked at the Barney Wharf. Steel published this picturesque postcard showing the ferryboat *Capt. John Smith* approaching Jamestown. (Courtesy of Annette Knoepfler.)

Judging from the smokestacks, there may be as many as five steamboats at the Barney pier in this 1907 photograph, when the 300th anniversary of Jamestown attracted thousands of people to the island. This photograph from an APVA annual report of 1910 is taken from Fort Pocahontas. (Courtesy of APVA Preservation Virginia.)

The 65-foot wooden ferry *Capt. John Smith* was built in 1924 by A.F. Jester at the Issac Hunley Shipyard at Battery Park, near Smithfield, and made her first run across the James River on February 26, 1925.

Capt. A.F. Jester put two smaller ferryboats in service: the *Pocahontas*, seen here, and the *Miss Carolina*. In 1945 Jester's ferry system was taken over by the Virginia Department of Highways and is today the only 24-hour ferry service in the state.

Captain Jester, almost indistinguishable in shadow, leans from the pilothouse window awaiting a deckhand's signal that all vehicles have been loaded and the ramp is ready to be lifted for the short trip across the James River. (Courtesy of Wallace Edwards.)

When Hurricane Hazel struck Jamestown in November 1954 the wind washed the Department of Highway's ferry *Miss Washington* up against the APVA's sloping seawall and left her stranded but undamaged. (Photo by Rodney Taylor.)

The most beloved of the James River steamboats was the *Pocahontas*, whose maiden voyage was on July 1, 1893. For the next 26 years she ran between Richmond and Norfolk, regularly stopping at two dozen river landings, including City Point, Newport News, Old Point Comfort, Portsmouth, and Jamestown. (Courtesy of APVA Preservation Virginia.)

A fire in the 1920s burned the warehouse at the end of the Barney Wharf, but ferry service continued with the use of the upstream loading ramp. Captain Jester constructed the small building at the foot of the pier as a waiting room. (Courtesy of Wallace Edwards.)

The majestic steamboat *Robert E. Lee* was cause for excitement as she docked the Government Wharf in 1948. One of those who ran to the pier to welcome her was Shirley Banks, who turns to wave at the photographer. Banks was a sales clerk at the APVA gift shop. (Photo by Rodney Taylor.)

The first steamship to dock Government Pier was *The State of Virginia* on June 15, 1929, which brought Maryland governor Albert C. Ritchie and 250 male members of the Eastern Shore Society from Baltimore. En route home, the Marylanders stopped at Old Point Comfort for a banquet in the Hotel Chamberlain. (Courtesy of APVA Preservation Virginia.)

In the summers of 1940 and 1941, Oscar Bohld, a colorful sea captain from Massachusetts, operated a naval training camp for boys aboard the *Marsala* that was anchored off Jamestown Island. The *Hull*, an Italian ship damaged in a hurricane off Cape Hatteras in 1938, was later taken over by the U.S. Maritime Commission and used as a refrigeration barge. (Courtesy of Colonial Williamsburg.)

Five

CEREMONIES

When Jamestown Day ceremonies were held inside the Old Tower Church in 1939, loudspeakers were set up outside so that the overflow crowd could follow the proceedings. That year the Right Reverend William A. Brown, bishop of the Diocese of Southern Virginia, conducted the service and Rep. David E. Satterfield of Richmond gave the principal address. (Courtesy of APVA Preservation Virginia.)

Assembled under a bower of pine branches on a flag-bedecked platform are participants of the 1895 Jamestown Landing Day celebration, which was held in front of the ruins of the Ambler House. Seated in the center is John Lesslie Hall, professor of English at the College

of William and Mary, and seated at the right with his legs crossed is Lyon Gardiner Tyler, the college president who initiated the annual observances on the island. (Courtesy of the APVA Preservation Virginia.)

The impressive gateway to the APVA grounds was built by the National Society of Colonial Dames who presented the APVA with a set of keys on May 9, 1907, four days before the 300th anniversary of the Jamestown settlement. The ironwork incorporates the society's coat of arms. The APVA's gatehouse was not built until 1929. (Courtesy of the Cook Collection, Valentine Museum/Richmond History Center.)

The date of this photograph of well-dressed visitors to Jamestown, reproduced on a postcard, is uncertain, although it is generally assumed to have been taken during the 1907 celebratory year. The principal events of the tercentenary were held at waterside exhibition grounds near Norfolk, and British ambassador James Bryce spoke at Jamestown for the May 13 observance. (Courtesy of APVA Preservation Virginia.)

Youthful descendants of Pocahontas and John Rolfe assembled at Jamestown in 1922 to unveil a statue of the Native-American maiden. Rolfe and Pocahontas, whose Christian name was Rebecca, were married in 1614 and the couple had one son, Thomas. Originally the statue was located near the entrance gate to the APVA grounds. (Courtesy of APVA Preservation Virginia.)

The shrine to commemorate the earliest celebration of Holy Communion at Jamestown was dedicated with appropriate ecclesiastical ceremony on June 15, 1922. It was erected by the Colonial Dames of Virginia and encloses a bronze bas-relief depicting the service that was conducted on the third Sunday after Trinity in 1607 by Rev. Robert Hunt, the colony's chaplain. (Courtesy of APVA Preservation Virginia.)

A masque—a form of dramatic entertainment based on an allegorical theme—was staged at Jamestown in 1935 by students from Williamsburg's Matthew Whaley High School to depict the spread of civilization in Virginia 300 years earlier. The girls on stage and those waiting to take their places represent the eight shires that made up the colony in the 1630s. Taking those roles were Pat Crutcher, Virginia Trice, Frances Wagener, Margaret Edwards, Virginia Garrett, Ruth Davis, Helen Vince, and Mildred Lapidow. On the stage at the right are students portraying various Virginia governors—Steven Holland as George Perry, James Bateman as Littleton Waller Tazewell, George Farthing as Sir William Gooch, and Gordon Lean as Sir William Harvey. (Courtesy of APVA Preservation Virginia.)

Celebrating Jamestown Landing Day in 1935 are, from left to right, the Right Reverend Arthur C. Thompson, bishop of the Diocese of Southern Virginia; state senator Robert W. Daniel; Mrs. J.B. Easter; Mrs. Granville Valentine, Virginia president of the National Society of Colonial Dames; Miss Ellen Bagby, chairman of the APVA's Jamestown committee; and R.A. Lancaster. Miss Bagby headed the Jamestown committee until her death in 1960. (Courtesy of APVA Preservation Virginia, photo by AP.)

Boy Scouts salute Virginia governor George C. Perry as he leaves the Old Tower Church flanked by George P. Coleman, left, mayor of Williamsburg, and Mrs. Perry after a memorial service on May 13, 1934. The state adjutant general, Brig. Gen. Samuel Gardiner Waller, is seen behind Coleman and Perry. (Courtesy of APVA Preservation Virginia, photo by *Richmond Times-Dispatch*.)

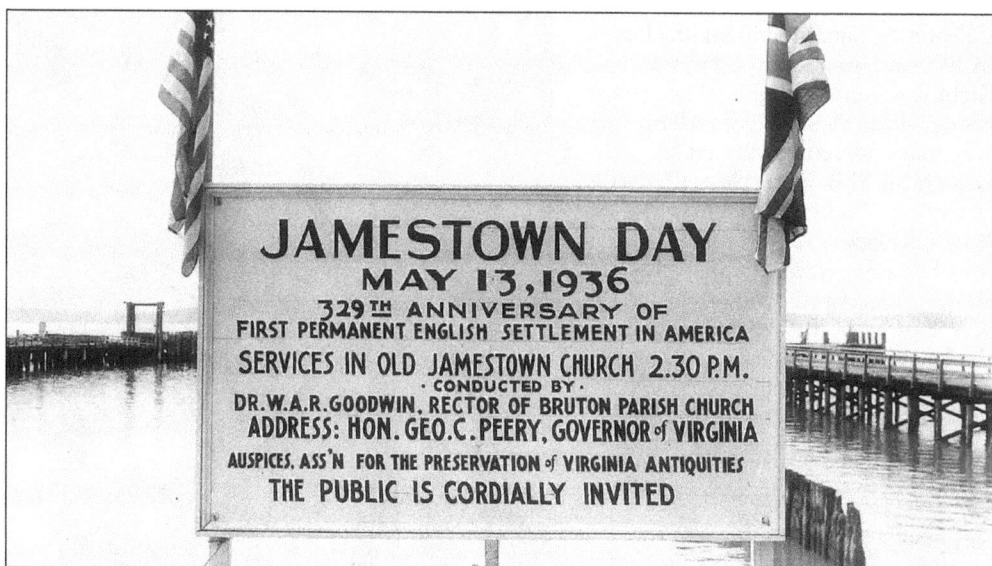

This billboard, decorated with American and British flags, was put up on the bank of the James Rivers between the Government Pier, upstream to the right, and the ferry pier at the left to promote the 1936 observance of Jamestown Day. Motorists waiting for the ferry to take them across the James River to Scotland Neck in Surry County could not help but see it. (Courtesy of the National Park Service.)

Among the several hundred persons who attended the 1936 Jamestown Day ceremony was Robert B. Yeardley of London, center, a collateral descendant of Sir George Yeardley, governor of Virginia from 1619 until 1621. With him are Rev. William Archer Rutherfoord Goodwin, left, rector of Bruton Parish Church in Williamsburg, and Gov. George C. Perry. (Courtesy of the National Park Service.)

On May 13, 1940, the famed aviatrix Jacqueline Cochran, here talking with Virginia governor James H. Price, came to Jamestown to pick up glass relics and fly them to New York City for exhibit at the World's Fair. The artifacts were found by Jesse H. Dimmick at Glasshouse Point where, in 1608, the colonists set up what has been considered America's first industrial enterprise. (Courtesy of APVA Preservation Virginia.)

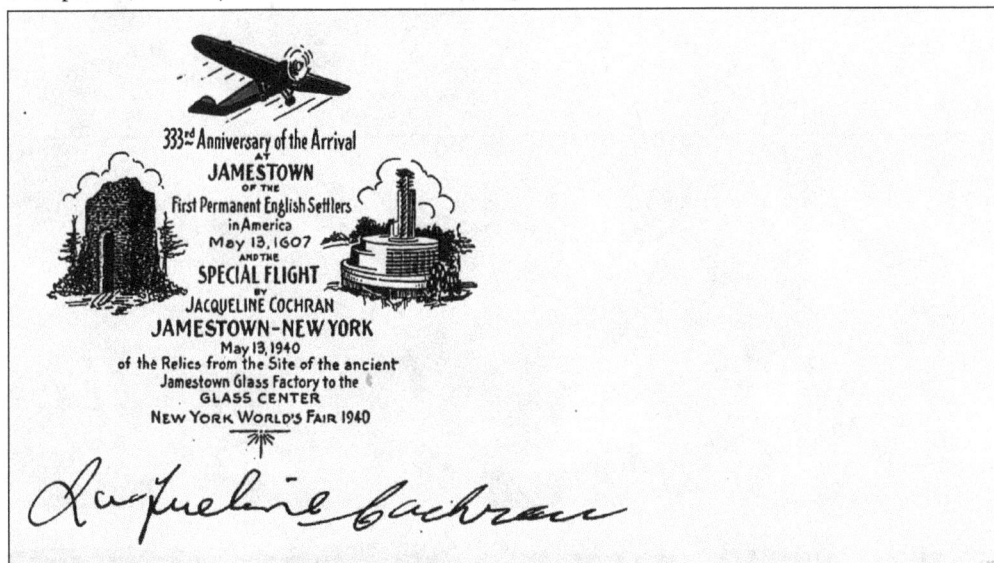

When Jacqueline Cochran flew to New York she took with her a sack of autographed cacheted envelopes to commemorate the occasion. The envelope carries a sketch of her plane flying above the Old Tower Church and toward the fair's Glass Center. She took off from the College Airport near Williamsburg. (Courtesy of Rodney Taylor.)

Rev. Dr. Churchill J. Gibson, left, chaplain of the Old Tower Church for the 1957 Jamestown Festival, officiates a reenactment of the 1614 wedding of Pocahontas and John Rolfe, portrayed by June and James Moffat, a married couple who held those roles in the outdoor drama *The Founders*. Assisting is Canon Selwyn Gummer, rector of St. George's Church, Gravesend, England, where Pocahontas was buried in 1617. (Courtesy of the *Virginia Gazette*.)

Ray Hilton, costumed as the captain of the guard at early Jamestown, opens the 1960 commemoration of the first legislative assembly in Virginia. On the platform, from left to right, are Gov. J. Lindsey Almond; Mrs. Almond; delegate Lewis A. McMurran Jr. of Newport News; an unidentified man; Rev. Cotesworth P. Lewis, rector of Bruton Parish Church in Williamsburg; and state senator Edward L. Breeden Jr. of Norfolk. (Courtesy of the *Daily Press*.)

Lt. Gov. A.E.S. Stephens of Smithfield, in the white jacket, also participated in the 1960 observance. Here he chats with delegate George Hill of Newport News, left, Ray Hilton and, state senator Fred Bateman of Newport News. (Courtesy of the *Daily Press*.)

Dr. Walter Muir Whitehill, director and librarian of the Boston Athenaeum, spoke at the 1966 Jamestown Day ceremony and praised the APVA and the National Park Service for protecting the island from commercial encroachment and bemoaning the intrusive development that engulfs Plymouth, Massachusetts. With him is Mrs. W. Taliaferro Thompson Jr., president of the APVA. (Courtesy of the *Daily Press*.)

Gilbert Cooper, mayor of Hamilton, Bermuda, recalls the colonial links between the British island territory and Virginia at the 1968 celebration of the first legislative assembly held in the New World. Sharing the platform are, from left to right, the Right Reverend John Bentley, former Episcopal bishop of Alaska; Lewis A. McMurran Jr., chairman of the Jamestown-Yorktown Foundation; Gov. Mills E. Godwin Jr.; Lt. Gov. Fred Pollard; and Speaker of the House John Warren Cooke. (Courtesy of the *Daily Press*.)

In September 1969 governors from Southern states convened in Williamsburg and on September 14 made a pilgrimage to Jamestown for an outdoor ceremony at the Hunt Memorial Shrine to mark the 350th anniversary of the first legislative assembly held in Virginia. (Courtesy of the *Daily Press*.)

Principal speaker for the commemoration of the 1619 legislative session was Lord Martonmere, the British governor of Bermuda, center. He is flanked by Virginia governor Mills E. Godwin Jr., at the left, and the Right Reverend David Rose, the Episcopal bishop of the Diocese of Southern Virginia. (Courtesy of the *Daily Press*.)

Perhaps the best-known Southern governor who attended the 1969 commemoration of America's first legislative session was Lester Maddox of Georgia, left, with his wife Virginia. Hosts for the conference were Virginia governor Mills E. Godwin Jr. and his wife Katherine, at right. (Courtesy of the *Daily Press*.)

Passing the costumed halberdiers on Jamestown Island are Delaware governor Russell Wilber Peterson and his wife Lillian, followed by Gov. Mills E. Godwin Jr. of Virginia. (Courtesy of the *Daily Press*.)

This trio of Southern governors is, from left to right, Preston Smith of Texas, Warren E. Heames of Missouri, and Buford Ellington of Tennessee. (Courtesy of the *Daily Press*.)

Six

FAMOUS VISITORS

Lewis A. McMurran Jr., left, chairman of the Virginia commission for the 1957 Jamestown Festival, presents a portfolio of photographs of the Virginia Peninsula to the Queen Mother during her visit to Jamestown. At the right is Robert Hatcher, chairman of the federal commission for the 350th anniversary of the Jamestown settlement. (Photo by Will Molineux.)

Elizabeth, the Queen Mother, poses before the statue of Capt. John Smith that looks out over the James River where he landed in 1607 as a member of the royally appointed governing council and, a year later, was named governor. The Queen Mother toured Jamestown on November 11, 1954. In 1960 she presented on behalf of the Commonwealth of Virginia a nine-foot-tall copy of the Smith statue to the city of London. It was placed in a park adjoining the historic Church of St. Mary-le-Bow in a section of the city Smith frequented. (Courtesy of Thomas L. Williams.)

Queen Elizabeth II reaches across the iron fence to shake hands with Sam Robinson, the longtime custodian and guide at Jamestown, after he recited his story of the Mother-in-Law Tree that grew between the graves of the Rev. James Blair and his wife, Sarah. While at Jamestown on October 17, 1957, the queen and Prince Philip, center, attended a brief prayer service in the Old Tower Church and were given a silver replica of a 17th-century Communion chalice and paten that was used at Jamestown. (Courtesy of Rodney Taylor.)

The Lord Mayor of London, Sir Denis Lawson, left, pauses on the steps outside the Old Tower Church while visiting on September 14, 1951, to talk with Ellen Bagby, who holds a small British flag. Immediately behind her is Lady Lawson. At the left is Rev. Churchill Gibson, the Episcopal chaplain for Jamestown. The sheriff of London, Lt. Col. J. Cullum Welch, holds a small Confederate flag; at the far right is Kenneth Chorley, president of Colonial Williamsburg (Courtesy of APVA Preservation Virginia.)

President Franklin Delano Roosevelt arrived on Sunday, July 5, 1936, at Jamestown by boat, coming down the James River after dedicating the Shenandoah National Park and visiting Monticello. His limousine stopped briefly at the Old Tower Church before going on to Williamsburg where the President, Eleanor Roosevelt, and Interior Secretary Harold Ikes attended a worship service at Bruton Parish Church and an afternoon dinner party at Carter's Grove Plantation.

Vice President Richard M. Nixon stands along the riverbank of Jamestown Island to witness the reenactment of the first English settlers to come ashore in 1607. At his side is Byron Hatfield, who wrote the pageant-drama staged on May 13, 1957, immediately after the ceremonial opening a mile upstream of Virginia's Festival Park. (Photo by Will Molineux.)

A delegation of congressman assembled at Jamestown in conjunction with planning the tercentennial celebration of Jamestown of 1907. In this postcard photograph they stand before Old Tower Church with its wooden sanctuary.

When this quartet of Episcopal bishops visited the Old Tower Church on October 5, 1907, the brick one had replaced the wooden church. They are, from left to right, the Right Reverend Alfred Madill Randolph, bishop of the Diocese of Southern Virginia; the Right Reverend Arthur Foley Winnington-Ingram, the lord bishop of London; the Right Reverend R.A. Gibson, bishop of the Dioceses of Virginia; and the Right Reverend Edo Jacob, lord bishop of St. Albans. (Courtesy of the Cook Collection, Valentine Museum/Richmond History Center.)

Norway's Crown Prince Olaf, center, and Princess Martha motored to Jamestown on the afternoon of June 27, 1939, and boarded a yacht to attend a mint julep lawn party at Brandon, the home of state senator Robert W. Daniel. Earlier, Prince Olaf, who was on a nine-week-long tour of the United States, stopped in Williamsburg and received an honorary doctorate of law from the College of William and Mary. (Courtesy of the National Park Service.)

Queen Frederika and King Paul of Greece visit Jamestown on November 23, 1953, while on an extended tour of the United States. Kenneth Chorley, president of Colonial Williamsburg, stands immediately behind the king. Ellen Bagby, chairman of the APVA's Jamestown committee, accompanies the royal pair. (Courtesy of APVA Preservation Virginia.)

King Bhumibol and Queen Sirikit of Thailand leave the Old Tower Church on a Sunday afternoon visit. Behind them is Carlisle Humelsine, president of Colonial Williamsburg. En route to the island their motorcade paused along the James River so the royal couple could have some private time walking the sandy shoreline. (Courtesy of the *Daily Press*.)

Thailand's Queen Sirikit pauses before the statue of Pocahontas, which, three years earlier, had been taken off its high pedestal and moved to the landward side of the Old Tower Church. The queen is escorted on her July 3, 1960, visit by Carlisle Humelsine, president of Colonial Williamsburg. (Courtesy of the *Daily Press*.)

Lady Nancy Langhorne Astor, center, the first woman to sit in British Parliament, was born in Virginia and in July 1947 she came to Jamestown to visit with two of her Richmond schoolmates, Ellen Bagby, right, and Lily Harrison Hill Bradbury, left. Lady Astor spent the night on Jamestown Island in the Yeardley House. She served in the House of Commons from 1911 until 1945. (Courtesy of Rodney Taylor.)

Stanley W. Abbott, superintendent of the Colonial National Historical Park, shows Virginia governor Thomas B. Stanley the National Park Service's commemorative Jamestown seal at the National Park Service's visitor center on Jamestown Island. The center was erected for the 1957 Jamestown Festival but will be replaced for the 2007 observance of the 400th anniversary of the settlement. (Photo by Will Molineux.)

Seven

RODNEY REMEMBERS

Jamestown Island was Rodney Taylor's backyard. When he was 12 years old, his mother Vivian and his stepfather William Harrison Smith moved from Ossining, New York, to Jamestown where, in September 1939, Smith assumed duties as superintendent of the historic grounds owned by the APVA. This photo of a barefoot Rodney and his mother was taken shortly after their arrival. All photographs in this chapter not otherwise attributed are from Rodney Taylor's family album.

Smith, who was a 13th-generation descendant of Pocahontas and John Rolfe, manned the APVA gatehouse and served as postmaster for the island and a rural area across the narrow Back River. Smith was paid $75 a month by the APVA but lived rent-free in a small cottage and was allowed "chicken and cow and garden privileges."

Vivian Smith assisted her husband at the gatehouse where, in this 1940 photo, she holds a sign advising visitors, "Enter Here Admission 25 cents." When Smith entered the navy as a lieutenant in 1942, Vivian took over as acting superintendent and as postmistress until he returned at the end of World War II.

The Smiths initially lived in the Godspeed Cottage—named for one of the three Jamestown ships—that was located behind the APVA's Yeardley House. Vivian Smith's father Willard Cypher of Ossining, New York, is pictured on the occasion of a visit. From 1942 until 1968 the Smiths lived in the Yeardley House.

Smith's mother and stepfather, Lily Harrison and Eugene Bradbury, lived for a short while in the Godspeed Cottage after they sold their farm near Upperville in northern Virginia. Here they take part in the 1946 Jamestown Day observance. The speaker is Virginia governor William M. Tuck.

The APVA road beside the Godspeed Cottage intersected nearby with State Route 31, the road that led northward to Williamsburg across Back River—or as the waterway was called in colonial times, the Thoroughfare. The Hurricane of 1933 lifted the wooden deck of the bridge

off its pilings, thus isolating the island. The deck was retrieved and replaced with the use of a crane mounted on a barge from Jack Tennis' sand and gravel business on the mainland at the left. (Courtesy of the National Park Service.)

Northeast winds at high tide frequently caused tidal flooding of the causeway through marshes on the mainland side of the bridge. Because the county school bus driver would not come on the island, Rodney had to wait for the bus at an abandoned shack at the northern end of the causeway. He skipped class the day in 1944 when this storm hit. Rodney graduated from Matthew Whaley High School in Williamsburg in 1945. The white post in the center is a gauge to mark the high water.

A few fishermen operated from docks along Powhatan Creek, which flows into Back River just upstream from Jamestown Island. This boat at anchor was owned in the 1940s by James Anderson. A few pleasure boats were also anchored there.

James Anderson, left, and William L. Tuttle, shown here preparing to cast off, fished for rock, shad, perch, and catfish, and trapped crabs in the James River off Jamestown Island. Tuttle operated a marine railway on Powhatan Creek where he repaired wooden boats.

James Anderson holds the tiller of the outboard motor while William Tuttle lifts their gill net to unload their catch. This snapshot was taken upstream from Jamestown Island and off what are now Jamestown Settlement and the Route 31 ferry pier.

Arthur Ayers, standing in the center, was the APVA's superintendent on the island from 1916 until 1935. He and his wife, Julia, fourth from the left and partially hidden, lived in the Yeardley House. Other members of the Ayers family lived on dairy farms along Route 31 in James City County. Standing behind Franklin Ayers and his wife, Mary, are, from left to right, Jane Ayers, James Ayers, Lowell Ayers, Julia Ayers, Nellie Gilley, Arthur Ayers, Floyd Ayers, Bessie Ayers, Lela Ayers, Ellsworth Ayers, and Ellsworth Ayers Jr. The little girl at lower right is Judith Ayers, daughter of Ellsworth. (Courtesy of Gayle Hensley.)

The APVA road from the Godspeed Cottage, at left behind the hedge of the Yeardley House garden, went across a meadow to Old Tower Church, behind the trees to the right and to the gatehouse/post office. In the distance is the Tercentenary Monument.

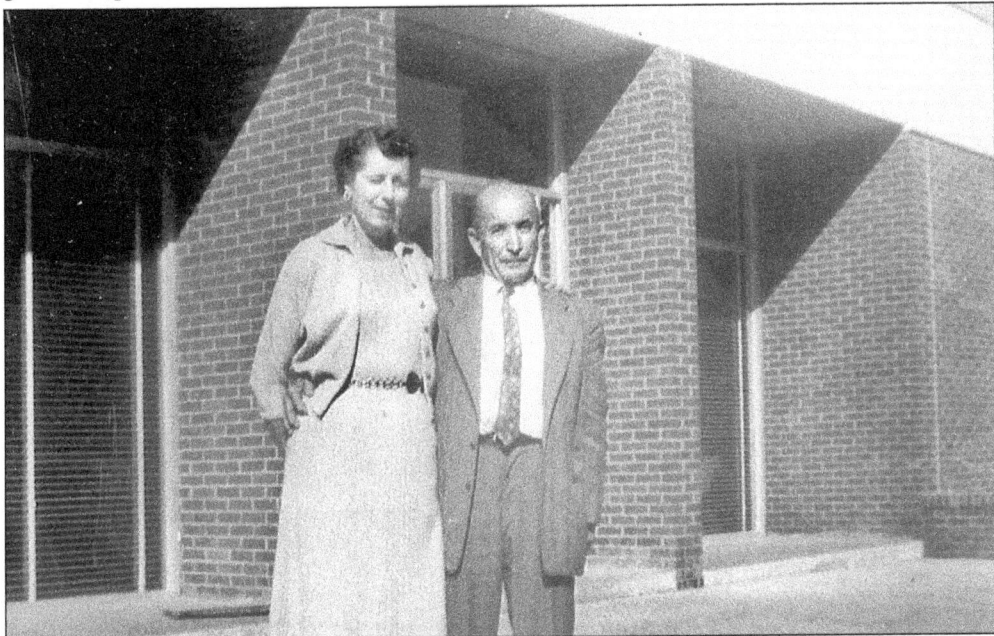

Ray Z. Mallory worked on Jamestown Island for the APVA as a maintenance man and groundskeeper from 1935 until 1960. He also helped out at the post office and gift shop. In this 1957 snapshot outside the National Park Service visitor center he is with Margaret Addison, a clerk at the APVA gift shop. (Courtesy of Ruby Thomas.)

Mallory was assisted by Richard Wilson, here chatting with an unidentified tourist. It was said that Wilson, when pushing his hand-mower, would follow good looking ladies around the island leaving unusual patterns of cut grass.

Carl Younglove managed the soda fountain and lunch counter in the building at the foot of the ferry pier and, over the years, held a variety of other jobs on the island. On the day this picture was taken in 1940 he had just rescued Rodney Taylor when his rowboat became stuck under the pier.

The soda fountain was an after-school hangout for Rodney Taylor, here a sixth-grader, as well as a gathering place for people living on and off the island. Eight families from across Back River routinely came to the island to pick up their mail.

Florence Jones was one of the clerks at the Jamestown soda fountain during World War II. The building was leased from the National Park Service by entrepreneurs. She lived across the James River in Surry County and commuted via the ferry.

The APVA seawall extended upstream to the confluence of Powhatan Creek and Back River opposite Glasshouse Point, in the distance on the northern shore of the James River. Here is where Rodney Taylor moored his rowboat. To the right an isthmus was created on which Colonial Parkway was extended in 1957 to Jamestown Island.

Sailing occupied a great deal of Rodney Taylor's boyhood interest and time. Here he sails downstream past the Capt. John Smith Monument.

The APVA owned a horse named Tom to pull a wagon and various farm implements. Here Vivian Smith passes a National Park Service ranger on the road to Black Point.

In the summer of 1946, after serving a short term in the Coast Guard, Rodney Taylor worked as a groundskeeper and drove Tom as he pulled a mechanical lawn mower. Rodney later served three years in the Coast Guard during the Korean War.

During World War II the army stationed a detachment of soldiers on the Government Pier to spot and identify all aircraft within sight. One of the servicemen was Vincent DeCicco of New York City, here with Rodney Taylor at the lookout shack.

Louis Rizzardi, a serviceman from Michigan, was another of the army's aircraft spotters. Their job was to telephone Coastal Artillery officials at Fort Eustis with a description of all aircraft seen in the vicinity.

John Clark, who came from Bayonne, New Jersey, liked to sail and he and Rodney Taylor often took a sailboat out on the James River. Clark was a talented artist and made sketches of the island.

The servicemen often helped Vivian Smith tend her Victory Garden. With her in 1943 in the Yeardley House rose garden are, from left to right, a private named Knight, Vincent DeCicco, and a sergeant from Maine named Blanchette.

The APVA gift shop was located in the Relic House, the porch of which is in the background. Taking a break between tour groups are David C. Davidson, standing; Becky Wells; and, holding an umbrella for shade, Rodney's maternal grandmother, Virginia Cypher.

One of Rodney's buddies in the Coast Guard was David C. Davidson of Kearny, New Jersey, who worked four summers as a sales clerk in the APVA gift shop. Here, in 1948, he is with Benchy, Rodney's dog. After Davidson retired in 1985 from the Summit, New Jersey, school system, he moved to Williamsburg and worked for Colonial Williamsburg.

William Harrison Smith, left, retired from the APVA in 1968 and from the post office in 1971. With him on the steps of the Yeardley House is his cousin, Pembroke Thomas, who served as curator at nearby Jamestown Festival Park until the 1960s.

Pembroke Thomas and his wife, Ruby Montgomery Thomas, lived in the Godspeed Cottage. Ruby was for almost 30 years an employee of the APVA. Here she poses at the well near the foundations of the Ludwell Statehouse complex.

One of the more popular postcards sold at Jamestown is this one of Okee, a 14-pound cat owned by Marguerite Stuart Quarles, who managed the APVA gift shop and considered herself as the hostess for Jamestown. In 1942 she moved to Richmond to be executive director of the APVA. Okee is an Indian word meaning "the one alone."

Posed on the same sundial in the rose garden of the Yeardley House is Puppy, Vivian Smith's cocker spaniel. The purebred dog is also officially registered as Rebel.

Eight

JAMESTOWN FESTIVAL OF 1957

One of the architectural features of the state's $1 million Jamestown Festival Park was this parabolic Information Center. Along with all other 1957 museum structures it has been replaced in anticipation of the Jamestown celebration in 2007. The park is now called Jamestown Settlement. (Courtesy of the Virginia Chamber of Commerce.)

A narrow spit of land was created in order to extend the Colonial Parkway to Jamestown Island, above, and State Route 31 was relocated upriver to lead to a new ferry pier, far to the right and not visible in this aerial photograph taken on November 16, 1956. A short new road, at the left, connects the parkway and the highway. (Courtesy of the Jamestown Foundation.)

Architects for Festival Park were Louis W. Ballou and Charles C. Justice of Richmond, and the general contractor was John W. Daniel of Danville. The relocated ferry pier is clearly visible, but trees hide the reconstructed James Fort, Native Village, and Jamestown ships. At the top of the mall is the Discovery Tower. (Photo by Thomas L. Williams.)

In March 1957, construction superintendents at Jamestown Festival Park worked out of a trailer, center, to rush completion of the Information Center, left; Mermaid Tavern, center; and Old World Pavilion, right. A covered walkway was built to connect these buildings and the New World Pavilion which was near the base of the Discovery Tower from which this picture was taken. (Photo by Will Molineux.)

The park opened April 1, 1957, too early to establish a lawn on the mall. The Information Center is at the left. Administrative offices and a gift shop are located under the flat roof. The Mermaid Tavern, named for a famous London hostelry of the 17th century, is to the right. (Photo by Will Molineux.)

The 1957 festival was directed by two commissions, one state and the other federal. Commissioners are, from left to right, (front row) Lloyd C. Bird, state vice-chairman; Samuel M. Bemiss, federal vice-chairman; Robert V. Hatcher, federal chairman; and Lewis A. McMurran Jr., state chairman; (middle row) Dr. Frank Boyden of the federal commission; and Edmund T. DeJarnette, Edward L. Breeden Jr., Felix Edmunds, and Fred Pollard, all of the state commission; (back row) Bentley Hite of the federal commission; Carlisle H. Humelsine of the state commission; Lt. Gen. Withers A. Burress, president of the Virginia 350th Anniversary Celebration Corp.; Parke Rouse Jr., executive director of the state commission; and Col. H.K. Roberts, director of the federal commission. (Courtesy of Thomas L. Williams.)

Parke S. Rouse Jr., left, executive director of the festival, and A. Harold Midgley of the British Central Office of Information are all smiles on the opening day of the Jamestown Festival. Midgley spent months in Virginia arranging the exhibits in the park's Old World and New World pavilions. (Photo by Will Molineux.)

Donald Harold, who came to Jamestown from Monroe, New York, was responsible for furnishing the reconstructed James Fort and Native village. At his elbow is Jeanne Etheridge, principal of Matthew Whaley School in Williamsburg. (Photo by Will Molineux.)

Visitors of the Old World Pavilion encountered a scale model of the English ship *Mathew* in which John Cabot sailed in 1497 with a crew of 18 to the northeast coast of America, permitting England to establish a claim to a share in the New World.

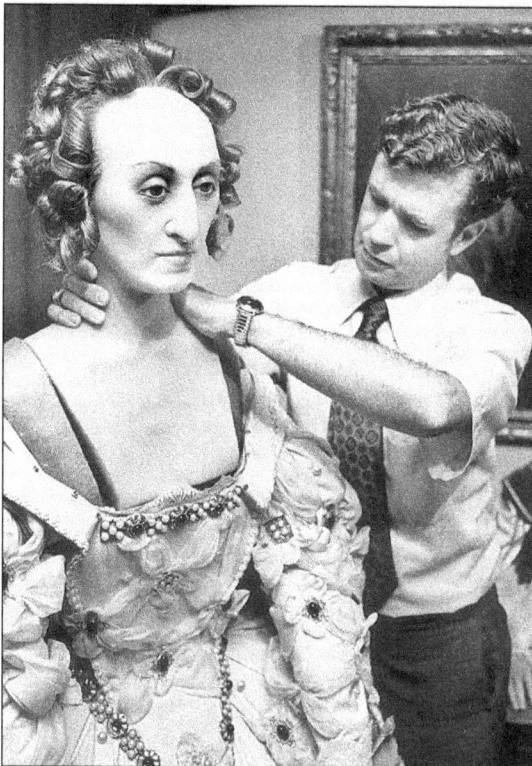

Dan Hawks, curator for the Jamestown-Yorktown Foundation, adjusts the gown on a mannequin figure of dour Queen Elizabeth I on display in the Old World Pavilion. The gown, a copy of the one in the Bitchley portrait of the queen, had been removed to be cleaned. (Courtesy of the *Daily Press*, photo by Mary Goetz.)

In the New World Pavilion visitors come upon a tableau of wax figures representing the Virginians who signed of the Declaration of Independence. The figures were made in England by craftsmen for Madame Tussaud's Wax Works in London. (Courtesy of the Virginia Chamber of Commerce.)

Mrs. Esther Ruffin of Williamsburg, who had been a senior Colonial Williamsburg hostess, was in charge of training guides for Jamestown Festival Park. She enlisted an enthusiastic corps of 70 people. (Photo by Will Molineux.)

When it was constructed in 1957, the triangular-shaped palisade of James Fort and the thatched-roofed dwellings it enclosed were thought to be an accurate representation of the original 1607 settlement, but subsequent archaeological discoveries seriously question both the dimensions and the construction techniques. The replica of the *Susan Constant*, the flagship of Sir Christopher Newport, is moored in a protective basin. (Courtesy of the *Daily Press*.)

The interpreters in the reconstructed James Fort presenting this idealized life-on-the-scene tableau are Hugh Hitchens, who applies mud-like daub to a wattle wall; Becky Smith, who impersonates Pocahontas; and Ray Hilton, who wheels a barrel of tobacco, portraying John Rolfe. (Photo by Chiles Larson.)

In this scene a friendly brave who joined a hunting party helps the colonists bring home to James Fort a buck supposedly gunned down by the lone colonist who is carrying a gun. The huntsman is Lyle Burroughs, a retired army colonel who was a guide at James Fort. (Photo by Chiles T. Larson.)

While two noblemen and their ladies stroll nonchalantly around James Fort one of the lesser sort struggles with a bundle of reeds to form a roof for one of the wattle-and-daub huts within James Fort. The first women arrived in October 1608 and this scene is somewhat reminiscent of cavalier times in colonial Virginia. (Photo by Thomas L. Williams.)

Inside Powhatan's Lodge, James Ware, a member of the Rappahannock tribe, looks over the display of animal pelts and baskets. The origin of the old dugout canoe is unknown. (Photo by Thomas L. Williams.)

James Ware stirs the ashes of a slow-burning fire as he works to hollow out a log canoe. A boy hidden the shadow of the small wooden structure mounted on poles rattles a gourd to frighten birds away from a seeded corn patch. (Courtesy of the *Daily Press*, photo by Mary Goetz.)

110

Few pictures can better illustrate the material difference between Europeans and Native Americans when they first met than this photograph of James Ware in his log canoe in the Festival Park's ship basin with copies of the square-rigged ocean-going vessels that crossed the Atlantic in the 17th century. (Courtesy of the *Daily Press*, photo by Mary Goetz.)

The replicas of the three merchant vessels that brought the English settlers to Virginia were built at Dunn's Marine Railway in West Norfolk in conformance with what was known about the size and rigging of, from left to right, *Susan Constant*, *Godspeed*, and *Discovery*. Anne Geddy of Williamsburg and an unidentified costumed interpreter pose for this publicity shot taken in the 1960s. (Courtesy of the Jamestown-Yorktown Foundation.)

Dressed in a sailor's uniform, a park guide points out the great cabin of the *Susan Constant*. The Jamestown settlers left England on December 20, 1606, and made landfall at Cape Henry on April 29, 1607. (Photo by Thomas L. Williams.)

A tug nudges the *Susan Constant* away from her moorings and out into the James River. This copy of Capt. Christopher Newport's flagship made several promotion trips before she was replaced in 1991 by a vessel made at Jamestown Festival Park. The original *Susan Constant* carried about 54 passengers and a crew of about 17. (Courtesy of the *Daily Press*, photo by Mary Goetz.)

This copy of the 68-foot-long *Godspeed* was made of hand-hewn timbers at Festival Park in 1984 and carried to England aboard a modern freighter for a return trip under sail to Jamestown. After battling a severe storm off Cape Hatteras, North Carolina, she arrived back at Jamestown on October 22, 1985.

The smallest of the three ships is the 38-foot-long *Discovery* with a cargo capacity of 20 tons. This replica of the 17th-century merchant ship is on sea trials in 1956 in Hampton Roads. (Photo by Walter Miller, courtesy of Jack Hiller.)

Several hundred people gathered at Jamestown Festival Park on a chilly April 1, 1957, for the ceremony opening the eight-month-long festival marking the 350th anniversary of the English settlement. Gov. Thomas B. Stanley is at the podium. The 80-foot-tall Tower of Discovery is in the distance adjacent to the New World Pavilion. (Courtesy of the *Daily Press*.)

Hatfield Chilson, undersecretary of the Interior, presided at the first flag-raising ceremony at Festival Park. Soldiers detailed from the First Battle Group at Fort Myer, Virginia, and dressed as 17th-century halberdiers, ceremoniously raised the flags of the United States, Great Britain, and Virginia every day of the festival. (Courtesy of the *Daily Press*.)

Vice President Richard M. Nixon addressed a large audience seated on the mall for the 350th anniversary of Jamestown Landing Day. Pat Nixon stands behind him as Gov. Thomas B. Stanley applauds and looks toward her. Models of Air Force jets are on the table in the foreground. (Photo by Will Molineux.)

Viscount Hailsham, British minister of education, brings greetings from the United Kingdom at opening-day ceremonies. He is standing in the park's Court of Welcome beside the Information Center. (Photo by Will Molineux.)

116

As director of pageantry for the festival, Byron Hatfield, left, relied on Capt. Ronald K. Irving to portray Capt. John Smith. Irving narrated reenactments of the several landfalls made by the English colonists before they settled on Jamestown Island. (Photo by Will Molineux.)

After the speech making, a picnic lunch was served to invited guests at the Mermaid Tavern, but there were not enough chairs and tables for everyone. These folks sit at the edge of a fountain with their legs stretched across a tulip bed. The Old World Pavilion is in the background. (Photo by Will Molineux.)

117

Gov. Thomas B. Stanley good-naturedly takes a turn blowing glass under the guidance of Ernest Tomlinson at the reconstructed glasshouse of 1608. The ovens, made from boulders from the riverbank, were manned in 1957 by craftsmen from leading American glass manufacturers. (Photo by Will Molineux.)

The same day that the festival began, an extension of the Colonial Parkway linking Williamsburg with Jamestown was opened. Cutting the ceremonial ribbon are, from left to right, Gov. Thomas B. Stanley; Frederick Mueller, assistant secretary of commerce; Viscount Hailsham; and Conrad L. Worth, director of the National Park Service. The ceremony in Williamsburg attracted the interest of patients of Eastern State Hospital. (Photo by Will Molineux.)

118

Three Air Force jet fighters, christened in London for the Jamestown ships *Susan Constant*, *Godspeed*, and *Discovery*, flew non-stop across the Atlantic and over Jamestown Island on May 13, 1957. Lady Clementine Churchill christened Maj. Charles C. "Buck" Jones' F-100 the *Discovery*. (Courtesy of the U.S. Air Force.)

A delegation of 115 Virginians led by Gov. Thomas B. Stanley (including two Episcopal bishops) went to England in October 1956 to invite Queen Elizabeth II to visit Virginia. They visited Brunswick Wharf on the River Thames, site of the December 20, 1606 departure of the Jamestown colonists, and heard remarks by Lord Waverley, chairman of the London Port Authority. The flags of Virginia and the Jamestown Festival rest on memorial wreaths.

Queen Elizabeth II arrives at Jamestown Festival Park on October 16, 1957, escorted by Virginia governor Thomas B. Stanley, on her right, and Ambassador Wiley Buchanan, U.S. chief of protocol, on her left. Prince Philip, the Duke of Edinburgh, follows accompanied by Mrs.

Stanley, to his right, and Mrs. Buchanan. Approximately 25,000 people saw the queen that day at Jamestown and later in Williamsburg. (Courtesy of the Virginia Chamber of Commerce, photo by Phil Flournoy.)

Queen Elizabeth II told a large audience on the mall that Americans and British "rightly cherish our diversities of character and tradition, but the fundamental concepts which have inspired both the United States and the nations of the Commonwealth are the same." Afterward she visited Jamestown Island and attended a brief service in Old Tower Church. (Courtesy of the Virginia Chamber of Commerce, photo by Phil Flournoy.)

Lady Caccia, wife of the British ambassador Sir Harold Caccia, raises the Jamestown Festival flag on May 13, 1958 to unveil a bronze marker commemorating the fact that it was at Festival Park the previous year that Queen Elizabeth II first addressed the American people. Assisting her is Lewis A. McMurran Jr. (Courtesy of the *Daily Press*.)

Queen Elizabeth II, while on a tour of Jamestown Festival Park, pauses at the recreated Native-American lodge to watch an unidentified woman demonstrate the traditional way Native Americans ground maize. With her is Virginia governor Thomas B. Stanley. Behind her animal pelts are stretched to dry. (Courtesy of the *Virginia Gazette*, photo by Merritt Ierley.)

The British ambassador to the United States Sir Harold Caccia and Lady Caccia peer into the cramped cabin space of the *Susan Constant*, a replica of the largest of the three ships that brought the Jamestown colonists from England. Sir Harold was a frequent visitor to Jamestown during 1957. (Photo by Thomas L. Williams.)

Dressed in his ceremonial robe, the Lord Mayor of London Sir Cullum Welch, on his 1957 visit to Festival Park, chats with halberdiers, all army enlisted men from the Third Infantry Regiment, the Old Guard. Escorting him, at the left, is Leslie Rowdon of the British Central Office of Information. (Photo by Thomas L. Williams.)

Tobacco farmers from across Southside Virginia gathered at Jamestown Festival Park on May 17, 1962, to salute the crop that economically saved the colony and the continued prosperity of Virginia's export tobacco trade. Hosting the event was Gov. Albertis S. Harrison, himself a tobacco farmer, who noted that "everyone is a beneficiary" of the tax revenue generated by those who smoked tobacco. (Courtesy of the *Daily Press*.)

Lacey Virginia Harrison, wife of Gov. Albertis S. Harrison, unveils a statue of Queen Elizabeth I draped with the Cross of St. George at ceremonies on May 17, 1962 at Festival Park. The statue, a copy of one in London that was made in 1586, was the gift of the American Tobacco Institute. (Courtesy of the *Daily Press*.)

The Spanish ambassador, the Count of Motrico, and the Countess Axacan, receive a sword salute as they arrive at Festival Park on November 10, 1957, to commemorate early Jesuit missionaries who lived briefly among the Virginia tribes as early as 1570. (Photo by Thomas L. Williams.)

In celebration of the first chickens in America, which arrived in 1607, the Virginia State Poultry Federation held a gala barbecue at Festival Park in 1957. Sharing in the fun are Vivian Smith of Jamestown Island and Lewis A. McMurran Jr., chairman of the state Jamestown Foundation. (Photo by Thomas L. Williams.)

Chief Oliver Adkins of the Chickahominy tribe lent his understanding of Native traditions to his interpretation of life in Virginia in the 17th century. (Courtesy of the *Daily Press*, photo by Mary Goetz)

Students across the state participated in hometown celebrations of Virginia's heritage during 1957. Bill Roberts, center, and Lloyd Sullenberger, both of Williamsburg, appeared as braves at one such event at Jamestown. The photographer is Will Molineux, then of The *Virginia Gazette*. (Courtesy of Ruth Roberts.)

127

Promoters of Jamestown Festival Park initially thought visitors might dress up to meet the costumed halberdiers in the reconstructed James Fort, as indicated by this 1957 publicity photograph of an immaculately dressed couple. (Courtesy of the Virginia Chamber of Commerce, photo by Phil Flournoy.)

Retired Maj. Gen. Bruce Easley, left, a member of the advisory board of the Garden of Patriots at Cape Coral, Florida, presents Lewis A. McMurran Jr. with a "History Happened Here" plaque in recognition of Virginia's commemoration of the nation's beginnings at Jamestown. The presentation took place on May 13, 1967. (Courtesy of the Jamestown Foundation.)

www.ingramcontent.com/pod-product-compliance
Lightning Source LLC
Chambersburg PA
CBHW050639110426
42813CB00007B/1856